On the Face of It

Maurice Lindsay is a well-known poet, broad-caster and prolific writer on many aspects of Scottish life and literature. He is the author of a much-praised *History of Scottish Literature* (now in paperback), *The Burns Encyclopaedia*, *Robert Burns: The Man, His Work, The Legend*, *The Castles of Scotland* and with Joyce, his wife, as co-editor, *The Scottish Quotation Book*, *The Music Quotation Book* and *The Theatre and Opera-lover's Quotation Book*. They have also edited together two other anthologies *The Scottish Dog* and *A Pleasure of Gardens*.

Maurice Lindsay's books include:

History of Scottish Literature
Robert Burns: the Man, his Work, the Legend
The Burns Encyclopaedia
The Castles of Scotland
An Illustrated Guide to Glasgow 1837
Collected Poems 1940-1990*

with Joyce Lindsay

The Scottish Dog
A Pleasure of Gardens*
The Scottish Quotation Book
The Music Quotation Book
The Theatre and Opera-lover's Quotation Book

*now available from James Thin, The Mercat Press, Edinburgh

On the Face of It

Collected Poems
Volume Two

Maurice Lindsay

ROBERT HALE • LONDON

ISBN 0 7090 5142 5

Robert Hale Limited
Clerkenwell House
Clerkenwell Green
London EC1R 0HT

*The publisher acknowledges subsidy from the Scottish
Arts Council towards the publication of this volume.*

Printed in Great Britain
by St. Edmundsbury Press, Bury St. Edmunds,
Suffolk and bound by WBC Bookbinders

CONTENTS

PREFACE

During the summer of 1992 there appeared what purported to be a scholarly survey of twentieth-century Scottish poetry, but in which the work of a number of well-known poets was not, in fact, included. A tabloid journalist, in search of possible copy, rang me up seeking my reaction to my own omission. The editor's personal preference, political predilection, lack of objectivity and narrowness of taste, I said, had nothing whatever to do with me. As it happened, I added, I had once written a fairly coruscating critique of that editor's early verse for an American publication. Being well aware of the bitterness of Scottish pseudo-gladiatorial poetic rivalries, I had not really expected to be included. Only when literary surveys are conducted from a calmer standpoint beyond the influence of living personality-clashes can objective definition be achieved. There was a long pause. 'What's that?' said the tabloid journalist. 'Not the end of the world,' said I; the proof of which is the appearance of this volume.

The poems that make it up have been selected from work written or revised between 1990 and 1993. Together with the contents of my *Collected Poems 1940-1990*, they would form the basis of any future *Complete Poems* - made ultimately necessary by the collapse of the Maxwell-owned Aberdeen University Press - with the addition of 'The Baffled Balladeer' (omitted from the Aberdeen University Press *Collected Poems* because in that particular context it might have tilted the balance too strongly towards the lighter verse section) and 'Elegy for an Actor Drowned in Time of War', unaccountably overlooked but subsequently included in the *Faber Book of Movie Verse*.

I am grateful to my friends George Bruce and James Aitchison for suggestions as to the final selection of these poems, some of which first appeared in *Interim* [USA], *Poetry Wales, Northlight, Lines Review, Chapman, Co-op Caring Poetry Anthology,* and *Stand*. The poems with bracketed dates in the list of contents are rewritten versions of older pieces.

I should like to thank Morven Cameron for permission to use the drawing on the cover of this book.

Dedication

(for Joyce)

For all our youthful passion's touching lust,
for children, for experience that banks
the years of loving to affectionate trust
shoring unsheltered age, my darling, thanks

JULY

It wasn't the tribal wars of long-dead kings
fighting embattled bigotry over lost ground
that made July the longed-for month to come round,
but the sweet deceiving a summer's childhood brings:
the scrabble of crabs, the breathing seaweed coast;
a house bracing its hundred years to the sea
that carried its builder's fortune, shipping tea;
a garden that couldn't care who gained or lost;
an open lawn like an invitation, stretched
through multi-partied borders hosting flowers
tashed with the scent of *now*; loose-petalled hours
stalking delight - a detached shadow etched
on memory; the scratch of a silent cry
behind the syllables of the word 'July'.

HIGHLAND WATERFALL

With shadow hands the clouds caressed two hills
divided by a gully. Rained-out spills,
oozing through sphagnum moss, the roots of ferns,
gathered their peaty coolness into burns
that pulsed and twisted to a running pace
momentum-high above a rocky face.

Beneath, I watched the weight of water falling
into itself, the roar to echo calling;
across the spray and spitter sunlight shone
fragments of rainbow broken over stone;
pieces of not belonging, flotsam-free,
with leaves and twigs frothed brownwards to the sea.

HIGH SEASON, OBAN

Sunlight semaphores the waving sea,
messaging Summer. Steamers slice the bay,
past hull-slapped, keeling yachts, sails belling free,
commotioned breezes rearing constantly.

A crawl of cars shuffles the crowded streets,
nosing some edge of vacant kerb to park;
pubs breathe out thirst; children suck ices, sweets,
while boatmen tempt town families embark
for island castles years have saddened grey,
yet flaunt the home-baked teas of holiday.
Then fish-and-chips, or dinner, candle-dark.

Crepuscular, the yellow baylight dusk
brings some to thrumming discos, some to walk
where seaweed, car fumes, cooking smells and musk
of gardens promenade in idling talk.

Hotels fall silent. Over sleeping peace
the mists of early morning spread their fleece.

THE RECORDS OF CIVILISATION

In an Orkney souvenir shop I bought a sweater.
The design's entirely based on local runes,
the shopkeeper told me. So I told my wife;
who told our grand-daughter; who was so impressed,
Mummy, she said, *Grandpa's given Grandma
a jersey bought in Orkney. It's all in ruins.*

SKARRA BRAE, ORKNEY

Parking opulent cars, we straggle across
the nearest field, wet with the wind's spittle,
peer through protective glass at the blenched remains
of folk like us five thousand years ago.

Difficult to imagine the short days passing;
the stone-bare tables, the lichened, strawy beds;
stunted hungers; the low unstooping lintels,
gnawed-at smokey meat or scooped-out shells,
the wind that never ceased gritting its sandy
message in from the sea above. Difficult
to imagine discussing brooches, the latest in skins,
charms to lessen the itch with, or numb the blowing
stench of discarded bones, the broken shards
of pots and beads; the rough-shaped hopes of things
lost irretrievably behind the beginnings
of language; sudden ruts of tender lust
that lent some warming brevity of trust.

CHRYSANTHEMUMS

Stiller than sheeted bed on which she lay,
over the bones of her face the skin stretched
tight, what she might feel or want to say,
lines of silence irretrievably etched.

Later, narrowed in her coffin, alone
with what once had been herself, I expected white
lillies waxing sympathy to be strewn.
Instead, chrysanthemums, their tongues alight,
shock-haired with requiem aeternam; whorled
heads burning autumnal flowers that curled,
consuming what remained in their acrid breath.

Whenever I see chysanthemums I smell death.

ANCESTORS

Bulging the covers of a pulpit bible,
the hinges of its binding bare with use,
my family - a history of tribal
wisdom and wars, example and excuse.

Foxed with the mouldered stains of vanished ages,
the names (with dates in brackets), ancestry
hanging the centuries across two pages,
like decorations on a Christmas tree.

My glance runs down - Mark, born in 1620,
to Matthew, died in 1969
at eighty-four, his latter bracket empty,
since no religion's left to string the line.

Lindsays who crossed from Normandy to settle
in Lennox, by the wild Loch Lomond shore
where kilted Highland caterans, reiving cattle,
pillaged and plundered through the Lowland door.

Lindsays to conquered Ireland bought their entry
as bonnet lairds astride a small estate;
aloof, brisk-riding Scoto-Irish gentry
who rode to law but fluffed the final gate,

yet struggled on till John, from Ireland driven
by bigotry to practice life assurance,
abandoned all the ghosts of those who'd striven
to cultivate what broke their long endurance;

the bitter soil successive Lindsays seeded
with colonising Scottish enterprise;
a hard, protesting race that never heeded
what Irish superstitions catechise.

Once back in Scotland, where the middle classes
ruled Glasgow through the remnants of its pride
in heavy industry, obedient masses,
caps tipping, passed by on the other side.

That order, settled privilege and money,
was shot to pieces in the war called 'Great';
kept-up overt appearances, once sunny,
felt pinched by shadows, cold and desolate.

My father, both humane and energetic,
counter of blessings who believed in thrift,
a business leader, publicly prophetic,
warned of the destination of our drift.

The unemployed, who bannered marching hunger
(passed in the streets by week-end motor cars)
broke draggled ranks, subservient no longer,
lounging by sullen doors of thirsty bars.

The right they starved for - jobs and living wages -
accelerated, touched by Hitler's war.
When peace at last redeemed its distant pledges,
mine was the face one ancient lineage bore.

Lindsays unnamed, anonymous as distance,
I celebrate you, lost in aimless time,
however briefly notching the insistence,
Maurice (born 1918) carved this rhyme.

IN THE DINING-ROOM

Hanging tinsel round the gilt of the frame
that scrolls Great-Aunt Matilda in her place,
for the first time I greet her, face to face.

Days filled with piety had been her aim,
we used to be told as, sternly, she would gaze
above our little heads at the green haze

of trees smudging the park. When old and lame,
she'd call, and if the servants weren't quick
enough, she'd rap the floor with her ebony stick.

Yet in her day she wore a borrowed fame
lightly, exchanging affluent social graces;
the Provost's lady who remembered faces;

the working classes, caged in poverty, tame
enough to nibble fingered charity
to salve the consciences of such as she.

Through growing years she watched whatever game
time got us up to. Shouting didn't vex
her, nor teenagers' fumbled sex.

Young adults, we reproached her as a name
that meant distrust of living, which we scorned,
sure in the confidence our senses earned.

To-day, if we still noticed her, we'd claim
the values she once stood for make-believe,
keeping appearances up, a leaky sieve.

Searching her settled gaze, it isn't blame
that shapes her lips, but *Is this all it's about?*
Great-Aunt Matilda, now I can share your doubt.

ON MILTON HILL

I: January

Snow wadges the silence of its white-out
over the hill, mufflering nearness in,
stitched criss-cross by the small feet of birds.
Distance crisps its calls through cleared air -
the thrusting churn of a rusty foreign.trader
shivering bent reflections through the river;
the railway's dickety-dack, the bark of a fox;
a farmer's tractor struggling against its will -
the shape of sounds made suddenly self-aware.

II: April

The cathedrals of the wind
are occupied by congregations
of clouds, singing
the drift of their own vacancy.

III: May

Great tongues of broom come licking down the hill,
as if the sun had had an overspill.

IV: June, Early Morning

The river draws itself off,
sifts into tiding sea.
Mud coppered by the sun
rests seagulls sheared of distance.
Grass radars low winds
hedge-hopping clear skies.
Hills riding rough-saddle
mile through the stretch of summer.

Idleness is hard to come by,
said an old Chinese poet*
one thousand years ago.
Letters lie, imposing questions

urgencies depend upon.
Such things do not change.
Reluctantly I turn away.

*Hsu Hsuan (916-991)

V: *August, Low Tide*

Hard by a dyke that shores encroaching land
the river drains its tide off, leaving sand

to glug and glisten naked to the sun.
A cloud, as if upon its final run,

swoops in, banks lower; turning inside out
it windbrakes on a shrill staccatoed shout;

the dangled undercarriage legs touch down,
a spread of white on what before was brown.

Grey-shadow-heads dip beaks through muddied brine
rippling the white sheet. On a given sign,

one bird picks up its corner to bestir
the fluttered edge of flight. With rustled chirr

the pattern reforms; the arrow whirrs,
smudging to clouded silence distance blurs.

VI: *December*

The low wind lacks strength
to clear mist from the valley,
left there inside out,
we above its lining.

Beads of moisture rivet
webs that link up leaves;
drips glub-glub from trees,
gutters trickle edges.

The air sags with moisture,
reluctant to be breathed.

DOORBELL RINGING

The dogs barked when I opened the door, flashing
the whites of their eyes to signal their suspicion.
Cleaner than clean, two young men stood there brashing
me texts of their Jehovah's Witness mission;
simplicities scrubbed fresher than their faces;
rootless promises floating on presumption;
naïvity put through disarming paces
with personable charm but lack of gumption.
As I reflected on what fiercely bites
such fellows with infections of belief
that mumbo-jumbo man-made verbal rites
thinking to lend mortality relief,
my dogs, denied a heavenly hereafter,
growled, being insusceptible to laughter.

TWO WORLDS
(for Siggy)

Out of what peaty sunken past you stare
at me, your recognising tail the sign
of contact made between your world and mine,
though where the other is, we're unaware;
you, nuzzling petting from the master's hand,
licking my ears awake, or curled in sleep
on my contented couch, although I keep
the ultimate obedience of command.
Yelping through fields of distance, you run free,
criss-crossing tracks that straggle wildness, tamed
by science; surveyed, analysed and named,
yet shadow-fences circumscribing me.
Brute instinct facing human thought; what binds
us, soft affection, ignorant of kinds.

IN THE TRAIN

Conductor, I said: *I'm afraid there's been a mistake.*
I asked for a seat facing the engine. They've booked me
one on the wrong side of the carriage. 'I'm sorry,
Sir,' the conductor answered. 'I'll change it for you.'
It's just, I said, *that I like to see where I'm going.*
I don't like being dragged through life backwards.
Smiling, he handed me back my punched ticket.
'Isn't that how it always is for most of us?'

MANNINGTREE

She boarded the commuter train with a few
companions, hair piled high like Nephertiti,
not caring who her sexuality slew,
a coldly classical face rejecting pity;
her contoured breasts and nipples sweatered tight,
a mini-skirt that curved her belly's round
and slightly parted legs, seemed to invite
a chosen lover breach her Venus's mound.
Opposite me, some preacher fellow read
his Bible, siding glances in her direction,
while I thought of the first time, naked in bed,
I staked my love upon a proud erection;
and sighed to think an old man's rage of lust
keeps love a memory held in fleshless trust.

GARDEN CENTRE

Gardeners speculate, wandering dwarf-hedged paths.
Sunlight winks their cars, as if in the know
how hard it is to persuade bought seeds to grow
the flourish on the packet. Plastic baths,
moulded for sunken pools, lie stacked like plates;
labels on roses flutter at hardy shrubs,
leading to fertilizers, sprays for grubs
and, beyond, the furniture, fences, seats and gates.
Commotioning their corner, a painted knot
of gnomes drop fishing lines that never go taut,
smirking with tweesome glee, as if each had caught
whatever answered the need his customer sought.
What they pull up's a different kettle of fish,
tangled with make-believing and rootless wish.

MR DOUGH, THE BAKER

Between the Gaelic hills and the village street
he baked night into morning, coaxed to lightness
his ordered loaves that rose to a daily whiteness,
crusted and mushroomed, breathing hot and sweet.

He looked, I thought, as God should, the dusty firing
finished, the labours of his six-day making
food for a seventh's rest, each Monday's baking
another need for satisfaction's tiring.

A card, some called him, but to me he seemed
a member of the Highland happy family
known, like my parents' house, or the pious homily
of fabled truths that through lost childhood gleamed.

Whenever I called at his bakery on the moor,
he served me more than a warmth of things to eat;
for he lived that sense of wholeness fields of wheat
swaying the valley had ears to listen for,
each wordless moment harvested, complete.

FIRST TIME ABROAD

The fact that you only managed an 'O' level English
doesn't matter at all when you go abroad,
said Mrs Ffolliat-Cholmondely to her daughter,
Serena. *Remember. Say everything slowly.*
Above all, speak with proper authority.
Loudly. Eventually, they understand.

There are excellent phrase-books, like this one here, to help
    you.
For instance: 'How is your uncle's health this morning?'
'Am I on the right road to the desert?'
'Excuse me, I think your camel is chewing my car,'
though perhaps these wouldn't help you much in Germany.
'I think there's something wrong with my undercarriage,'
useful where the roads don't come up to British
standards. And of course there's always culture.
'Are all the pictures owned by the Ministry?'
'Can you show me the way to the tomb of the old queen?'

It isn't so much what you say as the way you say it.
So long as you remember. Slowly and loudly,
even the stupidest foreigner understands,
since English is the language spoken in Heaven.

AT SEA

In the Bellevue Lounge, after a good ship's dinner,
watching the North Sea roll itself about -
a cloth the wind keeps reaching to pick up,
but can't - I thought of chartless Vikings rowing,
rowing, only the flickered points of stars,
light-years away, to guide them rumoured distance;
the smell of raw hide, rough words, rotten meat
the urine stench, salt-pitted swords, the whiplash
gales tearing the thongs that tied the sails,
sweating sinews; for all that, many a low-
thwart longship lost, sunk in a gulping trough

that over-swallowed. After weeks at sea
a blackened smudge rain-clouding the horizon
but slowly drying out to shapes and colours;
hard-driven keels crunching a stretch of sand;
huzzahing up the beach the lusts of conquest,
fresh food, the quaff of drink, then women, women . . .

Later, a played-out pianist returned
to skitter dribblings, stale sophistications,
beer slopping the tables. A tannoyed voice
announced when we'd arrive. Punctually,
the certainty of land rose up to meet us,
the measured edge of distance. I glanced through
my sheaf of conference papers, yawned, got up
and bought a final whisky, duty-free.

CHURCHGOING BRETON WOMEN

Coifed on top of grey-worn, gathered hair,
their lace-white piety's a wedding cake
briding them back to church to take the host
of weathered pardons, crafted here to make
the Christian story still a Celtic thing;
rocks blessed by the sea; the smell of fish
legending harbours; heathers from the moor
scenting a saint for every need or wish.

We tourists, holidaying unbelief,
marvel that here's the resurrected ghost
of antique holiness; pillars of air
staunching a roofless faith where peasants bring
praise to the God of storms; a dogmatist
whose stiff forgiveness grants them sole release,
certainty where no certainties exist.
We shudder. Better stay alone, unsure,
than share such frozen fantasies of peace.

FROM HERE TO HERE

Roaring to race the runway's gravity,
twin-engining a raising force, we angle
up, bisecting flight-paths of slow birds;

ribbons of roads, tied rails, recede together,
interstices accustoming directions,
transactions, taxes, secret deals, debts, credits;

chequered irregular fields, splodged trees and mountains
that blown-out winds tore with their ragged edges;
through fusilades of white, careening clouds

squadroning rain-storms to their next engagement,
we break into the golden fleece-lined blueness
the sun gilds half-a-round's clear distance with.

We page through novels, finger magazines,
Skyways, High Fliers, blondes on naked beaches
left stranded by the tides of paper sex;

watch others head-turn sideways, flashing eyes on
the rise and fall of the close-fitting bosom
a girl, relaxed, unguards across the aisle,

thinking how she'd do everything with style;
elbow through meals on mini-trays; half-stare at
a film about an all-American teen-age

tamed clean to goodness by his baseball coach;
glance through a cabin window - peeling darkness,
the moon slivers the rind of its own mass -

chat to the man beside who caps fired oil-wells,
the woman to the right who genteels music;
then lace the flight's soft thrumming with half-sleep.

Wakened, we fumble stickily a bun
and coffee, join the toilet queue to freshen
the travel from our faces; then await

the slide down sixty slanting miles, earth-surfaced
with sky-rinsed mountains, starry-coloured fields
and toybrick houses cotton-wooling smoke;

with insect cars that crawl to wait to greet us.
We lump along the runway, disembarking,
warm in the climate of expectancy,

to intimacies we were never part of;
invested, untranslated energies
hinged, much as ours are, on self-shadowed fears.

For here and everywhere live their own *always*:
what's different is the cut and shape of clothing
experience packs, the luggage of our minds.

IN CYPRUS

At the birthday party of a boy of five
he'd never met, and wouldn't see again,
he thought: 'If Mario were still alive
with such a run of years as his, by then
it would be twenty sixty-one. Would Serbs
be feuding blood against their neighbour Croats?
Would Turks and Greeks be sharpening the barbs
of edging similarities? Would votes,
bargained by statesmen, keep a buffered hold
on tribal certainties urging them kill
women and children in a different mould
of superstition, faithed by human will?'

Across the wide verandah, sunshine flaked
powered mimosa, baked surrounding scrub;
old Homer's curly-headed sea unslaked
its heaving shoulders lazily to rub
wet shadows on the rocks; its fabled rage
stroking the shingle, pulling back rinsed claws
gently, as if to show that it could cage
the stormy fury of its pointless cause.

IN DUBLIN
(for Tim O'Driscoll)

As I walked out through Grafton Street
I saw a sight you wouldn't meet
in Scotland if a month of Sundays
stretched to a century of Mondays:
a young man with, around his neck,
a placard telling you, on spec,
he was prepared by rote to say
as many poems as you might pay
him for. He listed Yeats -
by far the greatest of his greats -
Kavanagh, Muldoon, Seamus Heaney
The Irish Garda, not being meany,
strolled by to show that no one bothers
what harmlessly may turn on others
when people choose thus to rehearse
the pleasures of well-spoken verse
here, in a land where poetry's
a stuff to share with you and me.

I wondered what would happen if
a youth stood up and, to the good
and great of Edinburgh's High
Street said - not that *The End is Nigh*
(such pious rubbish is accepted
when said in place; indeed, protected;
Free Speech, they call it) - not for free
but for a very modest fee,
he'd speak MacDiarmid's lyric rhymes
in Scots; or, out of later times,
Liz Lochhead in her old man's hat
(whatever next will she be at?);
MacCaig, Smith, Lindsay or George Bruce;
or concrete Eddie Morgan, spruce
in fashion's avant-gardest suit.
Some boot upon another foot
would lash out insults like 'elitist'
(which really means the best and neatest
way that a thing can be achieved;
but teaching's now so misconceived

the best's thought stuffier than the worst,
the latest easy least put first.)
Police would appear to urge him on.
Advertisements should rest upon
an A-board which must have two flaps,
a front and rear, with shoulder straps,
and must keep moving through the streets,
like constables upon their beats.
They'd threaten the Fair Trading Act
since what he offered wasn't fact
that could be measured out and weighed,
tested for density, assayed;
then, all else failing, run him in
for making a malicious din,
breaking the peace.

              There's no condition
in Scotland so invites perdition
as showing off in public places.
We move about with narrow faces
like all true Calvinistic races,
rarely, if ever, kicking traces
the Irish shattered in their stride,
breaking a rule that meant divide;
and worry, after years of Union
with England's rollering dominion,
about our self-identity -
are we a national entity,
or just a folksy region losing
distinctiveness by our own choosing?

Well, here in Dublin I'm past caring
while for a coin or two I'm sharing
enjoyably the sound and sight
dead poets fashioned from delight.
Whoever makes or breaks the laws,
affirming life's the poet's cause.

IN AMERICA

I: *Watch Your Step*

The spread of Aids among the young is alarming,
an American TV voice declared. *Too many*
youngsters still don't seem to be aware
what causes it. On the television screen
a clean-limbed nice American boy, perched
on the end of a bed, is pulling on his sox.

II: *The American Way of Dog*

I want you to make a smart coat for my dog,
the lady said to the tailor. *Here are his measurements.*
Maam, the tailor said to the lady; *it sure would be easier*
if you just brought your dog in for me to measure.
But I couldn't do that, the lady said to the tailor,
It's meant to be a big surprise for him.

III: *A Rich American Lady*

She wore dissatisfaction like her make-up,
etched by the rise and fall of stocks and shares:
the slightest fluctuation seemed a shake-up
to catch her man-of-business unawares.
Three times a day she'd bid him buy or sell
before her millions fell below the line:
the worry of it kept her so unwell,
on pills washed down with potions she would dine.
She never breached the core of satisfaction,
but reined herself upon a cold reversal
to contemplate her next enforced inaction.
Life was for her an endless dress rehearsal,
the only show from which she hadn't shied
surprising her upon the day she died.

IV: Going Down

Driving over the Golden Gate bridge
    at San Francisco, the guide said
      it's over four hundred feet
        to the Bay below.

The water is cold and shark-infested,
    which is why
      nobody ever escaped from Alcatraz
        except Clint Eastwood.

(Police car lights flashing, the inner lane coned off.)

Uh-huh, it looks like somebody's just jumped.
    They do it regularly
      There's talk about
        putting a net beneath.

Fact is, if they don't jump from here,
    they'll jump somewhere else.
      So why spoil
        the look of a good bridge?

They get a good view of San Francisco
    going down.
      But it's too late then for them
        to change their minds.

V: For Howard Nemerov (1920-91)

You were my favourite American poet,
manipulating forms, and sometimes, rhymes;
bridger of sense across the sad inchoate
uncertainties disordering our times.
You fashioned tropes from syllabled confusion,
shaping your sanities out of what divides
the cant of creeds, the motives of illusion,
between the mad ones and the suicides.

'It's not the tune,' Bach-loving, you suggested,
that matters, 'but the turns it takes you through.'
Though now the urge that drove your music's rested,
point-counterpoint, your ring of words runs true;
there to delight whoever sounds your pages
when silence will have paid your critics' wages.

THE GULF WAR

I: *Read His Lips*

The best soap-opera we'd ever seen
on television, though it wasn't suds
that flowed when rockets failed to meet the Scuds,
or pilots roared the darkness off our screen,
or bombs breached targets and the streets between,
or knocked-out tanks lay belching twisted flames
as generals, accustomed to war games,
explained with diagrams what it should mean.
A victory. The ruined country free.
But what it meant, it turned out, was quite other.
A tyrant left with genocide to smother
tribes who took up their challenged liberty
half-promised by a politician's word
the unsaid half of which declared absurd.

II: *Thank God*

Tears that release a bleaker misery
than ever wept before, cry out aloud
through glass as nightly TV viewers see
what conscience cannot square; the huddled shroud;
old women on all fours, their ebbing strength
crawling to greet their death, while babies suck
the breasts of withered mothers, on a length
of frozen mountain-miles starved out of luck;

tears trickling from a noble tribal face
protesting to the world their only crime,
fleeing the genocide against his race
a tyrant practises a second time.
Help us! they plead, while politicians pray:
Thank God for granting us the victory.

III: *Uncomfortable With*
(On Thanksgiving Services for Victory in the Gulf War)

Give thanks to God! A famous victory,
prelates and priests go chanting through the land.
Honour the brave - with that we'd all agree;
but what is strangely hard to understand
is why the God the British middle classes
thank for protecting them should leave in place
a murderous dictator killing masses
who through a different route of faith seek grace.
Doesn't your God accept that souls of Kurds
are worth enough again to intervene?
Or could it be your unctuous whinge of words
makes self-deception verge on the obscene?

TOYS ARE US

Pop, goes the toddler's cork on a short string;
crack, smokes the pistol's cap in schoolboy fun:
a feathered pellet flies with the rifle's *ping;*
death grape-shots from a double-barrelled gun
on wild, defenceless things. Toy soldiers bring
legends to by-gone battles, lost or won.
Grimed actors in heroic poses sing
of battle's glories, enemies on the run.
We zap and splat each other in war games,
watch cops and robbers on the TV screen,
ambivalent as sometimes are their aims;
there's nowhere violent that we haven't been.
Fantasy playing real, for good or ill,
thus finds us well prepared. We'll shoot to kill.

LEAVE OF ABSENCE

Lushed in the Sussex Downs an old bewildered lady
greeted me hospitably, showed me around her house,
except for a locked room at the darker end of a shady
corridor. *No one goes there*, the surviving son would grouse.

But he took me up two whiskies after she'd gone to bed.
It's forty years since my sainted brother came home on leave.
Recalled to France in a hurry after the Somme, he said.
Killed. She won't accept he's gone. Refuses to grieve.

He led me up old stairs creaking of country night.
There's no electricity. His room was never wired
when the rest of the house was done. We have to use candle-
light.
He struck a match on the silence. The wick of the flame
    spired,

slowly the door squeaked. A fragile flickering blushed
yellow as illness, over the tossed-back sheets of a crumpled,
unmade bed; pyjamas rotted into the rushed
discarded strip he'd dropped them off in. The comb that
had rumpled

its drag impatiently through the hasty wave of his hair,
greased with uprooted strands, lay by the cracked stub
of his shaving stick, the open razor rusted. Layer
upon layer of dust encrusted the empty iron tub

that gestured his bent-up nakedness with splashing
circles of servant-carried water staining the floor;
anonymous shapes of action left by an officer dashing
off to a telegraph summons, a war at death's door.

There was nothing I could say, so in silence we descended
back to the fireside's living warmth and the whisky's glow;
yet that hurried ghost from the Great War supposed to have
    ended
war, blown to purposeless pieces all these years ago,

has haunted me ever since. The place has been torn asunder,
rebuilt as a playroom where the family fight war games
on the television screen and the zapped explosions thunder
only competitive laughter from electronic flames.

Victored and vanquished children equalled, tucked up in bed -
the battlefield switched off and put in its box away -
don't score their wars in terms of men on rations fed
who wont take up their places to fight another day.

But after the re-assuring light-out goodnights are said,
deaths that are for real slump before adult eyes
on the self-same screen; soldiers from rival armies, led
into a causeless country whose passport stamp is surprise.

TO ONE WHO REPROACHED ME FOR LAMENTING
THE DESTRUCTION OF OLD BUILDINGS

A tribal soldier aims, eyed by a television
camera; fires. The onion dome of a church
topples into its own dust, yards away.
God, it seems, has little enough to say,
having been left in an ages-ago lurch
as history unfolds its mindless mission.
Their soldiers behave like cruel animals, say
both sides. But animals don't kill,
except to eat another's hungered death.
We, with self-knowledge edged upon our breath,
and thundered blind with reasoning, can't will
a choice where no one's left with pain to pay.

Blame it on apples if such legends ease
your conscience, and no feminist Eve
proclaims the serpent's harrassment was male.
The tree of knowledge bends before the gale
as change keeps drifting and the shifts deceive,
till what seems right's the easiest to please.

So threatened mediaeval buildings make
us rage more than the razing of our kind,
art's values seeming nearer permanent;
the only objectivity we're lent
since human nature's wired and deeply mined
with hates exploded blood can never slake.

UNSAID

The other day I found myself at a wedding
where, sixty years ago, in the family pew,
Sunday after Sunday I sat there, dreading
boredom, the weekly sermon's rendezvous.
Yet, down from his pulpit, the kindly minister, treading
solemnly to the lectern where there lay
an enormous Bible, held me, suddenly spreading
poetry beyond what the words could say.
Now, a Committee, seeking clarification,
has carefully extracted mystery;
dried the great business waters from the sea;
pared down such wishful meaning that what shows
can't be believed in, stripped to naked prose.

ON THE FACE OF IT

Changing the channels on the T.V. set
alone in my hotel, flashed images
companion me: a strutting Spanish Hamlet,
a football field's goaled ecstasy; the scrimmages
of buttocked rugby churning foreign soil;
the news - in French; a stretch of suntanned boobs;
two flare-lit strugglers capping gushing oil;
advertisements for crisps and toothpaste tubes.
Externalised, a stream of consciousness
that parallels what fills the human mind;
half-thoughts that fade as vacancies digress,
distracting what the heart keeps undefined.
Playing at God, I press the switch-off knob;
and life recedes, a disappearing blob.

THE STATE OF THE ART

I enter Something House, in the heart of the city;
glass doors open respectfully, seeing me come.
A trim receptionist, scented something pretty,
stops titivating nails. A twittering hum;
rings Ms Somebody, on a higher floor.
Would I mind waiting? Barely above the ground,
a chromium chair squats, leering up. I lower
myself, am grasped by a sucking sound.
He'll see you now, a manicured voice declaims.
I struggle to level her patronising grin,
follow a wiggled bum that a tight skirt tames
to a muzaked elevator. It breathes us in,
swoops to the seventh floor. An officious *ping*
opens a gap. Handshakey Mr Thing.

So sorry you had to come, the ushered greeting
seats me lowly behind an enormous desk
in a room where polished words and the central heating
get a glassy bird's-eye urban view; grotesque
asbestos pipes, humped water-tanks, and the slates
of older properties speckled with coloured patches.
The trouble arises over a question of dates,
explains Mr Thing; *since once a computer latches
on to wrong information , it's hard to trace
the source of the error from which it drew its conclusion.
A matter of wrong identity in your case -
a man of the same name led to its confusion.
Lived in the same street. Dead for twenty years.
We've buried him now. You needn't have further fears.*

With that, Mr Thing rose up on his pinstripe feet.
You owe us nothing. It was the computer's mistake.
(The poor computer, I thought. Will it now entreat
forgiveness for all the worry that laid me awake
night after night, when it should have been haunting the
dead?)

'Did nobody bother to check the wretched machine?'
It's not as easy as that, he knowingly said.
'It makes me feel as if I had somehow been!
Another man of the same name!', I explained.
He flicked a smooth lapel. *It's the state of the art.*
We rely on computers, so nobody can be blamed.
Downwards I slid, a well-oiled frictioned part.
The receptionist smiled, as at someone she used to know
from *Who Was Who*, but who passed out long ago.

KEEPING IT CLEAN

We criticise the Spaniards for torturing horses
and tormenting bulls to satisfy their blood-lust;
yet flex the hypocrisy that coldly rehearses
arguments in favour of boxing; adjust
our po-faced consciences so that it's quite OK
for one over-muscled brute to batter another
senseless - the manly pastime, anchors aweigh!
KO'd to hospital, nauseatingly smother
his life-support machine with flowers by the hour
and prayers for his recovery. *Every game
has its risk. He hit his head upon the floor.*
Banning would drive it underground, proclaim
the pursey promotors. *Let the sport be seen.*
Just tighten the rules a little. Get what I mean?

BURNS IN DUMFRIES

Here he moved and had what you'd call his being,
the smells of dirt and beer clinging to narrow wynds
that welcomed him when, taxed with excising miles
he left his horse in the corner of his mind's

preoccupation, to drink himself to his fellows,
soothing the degradation foosty barrels
dunted him raw injustice with; forgetting
the barked knuckles, the puppified drawing-room quarrels

and the song that dirled his blood but couldn't be written,
only acted out of. As if he'd bet
the God he half-believed in that, without reins
and saddleless, he'd ride the white-thighed sweat

of shying, eager, red-checked Dumfries fillies
a gait where lords and lawyers couldn't meddle;
he who was up and away both man and master,
whom poverty couldn't catch in time to peddle

his pride for lost discretion. Remorse! Remorse!
systole and diastole, his heart kept pounding,
back to the generosity of his Jean
who patiently waited for him, never rounding

the whips of her anger on him, ready to bear him
over what gentler canter he needed next;
unsure of herself and his clever friends, content
to be what he always returned to, and only vexed

that he couldn't find whatever it was he wanted.
But what he found, oh the pity of it all!
left her behind in labour, and he not able to hear
the town band shakily playing the Dead March from *Saul.*

ENVIRONMENTAL AWARD

We descend on the district. Muncipal cars
purr us into a drab monotony;
street after street, as far as the eye can see,
stretchlands of architectural cadavers.

What's there for praise to judge? Hard to perceive.
Peeking guardedly, pinned-up curtain laces,
'the likes of them' pronounce identical faces.
From self-same doors the self-same women leave,

haplessly decent, prematurely sere,
lost causes like dead leaves swept up for burning;
as if from the same errand, each returning
by gap-toothed fencing - every stake a spear

for gangs to rip up war with - separating
tufts of cat-piss grass from ordered plot,
the houseproud from the couldn't-care-a-jot;
hard by our feet, stray mongrels copulating.

We talk among ourselves, give zero votes,
commend the effort uniformly mapped,
secretly thankful that we aren't trapped
as they are - we don't put that in our notes -

then, feeling vaguely guilty, though of what
we aren't sure, rejoin the limousines
and glide back to our safe, familiar scenes
where wounds get healed and hope's more cheaply bought.

CELEBRATING THE FORTH RAIL BRIDGE

This was the last land-challenge, linking Highlands
and Lowlands, losing lives to conquer space,
the smoke-plumed engine trellising its tubing,
invention mastering the sense of place.

This was an age that strove to reach perfection,
and thought it had, more confident than ours,
although its close assurances grew sated
with certainties that undermined its powers:

draining half-empty continents of profit;
missionising its own shapes of belief;
downing resistance; shabby tunes of glory,
administrative unction its relief.

Upwards, the challenge of the thrusting mountains,
cloud-paring, razor sharp, the highest ridge
beyond which none would surely call in question
the gap of heaven only prayer could bridge?

But birds flew vague, resistless destinations,
their feathered nearness shrinking *there* from *here*;
so emulating generations modelled
winged cabins thrusted through suspending air.

Now, a slow diesel trundles history
across a bridge still monumenting pride,
while far beyond the surface 'planes are arc-ing,
spaceships and rockets probe the last divide;

receding stars, the edgelessness of nothing,
what holds together time's constricting laws.
If life has meaning, what was its beginning,
a clutch of rival gods, the uncaused cause?

Much-painted link of elbow-stretching girders,
more than the mere conveniency it spans;
a milestone left magnificently marking
the destiny of searching that is man's.

Any more for the 'Skylark'?, a comical old man bawls
at the river's edge as the ropes of holiday
splash loose, and the chugging vessel slowly crawls
free of her river moorings, blunting Loch Lomond spray
as she gathers speed through waters the wind scrawls
with forgotten Gaelic legend; names that the mountains say,
though soapsie television's high road calls
new tunes the happy-go-luckers pipe to-day.
Fifty-one years ago, he mused, *she braced
herself across the besieged Channel to reach
Dunkirk. She ferried soldiers high and dry
to fishing-boats and paddle-steamers spaced
in deeper waters. Those of us there on the beach
heard, 'Any more for the "Skylark"? ' It bloody near made me
cry.*

PRODUCING *DON GIOVANNI*

I

They have torn the nineteenth century interior
out of the theatre - the plutocratic plush,
heavy with Hapsburg women, stale cigars,
velour thread-bared by smug capitalist bums -
replacing it with replica; as it was
in 1787; the October evening
when Mozart stood before the orchestra
and raised his hands to begin *Don Giovanni*
Just as it was - except for electric candles -
seats, hangings, rococo decoration.

Pity they hadn't a reproduction Mozart.

II

Here's this guy, struggling to get the pants off
an aging broad his dumb friend plans to marry.
Irate father rushes to intervene;
the boyo plugs him straight between the eyes
with a small machine-gun, masking his escape.
He's got women on the brain (and other places).
Those he's discarded mix with dressed-up cops
at a kind of fancy ball. They plan to arrest him;
but what with the champagne and all that singing,
once again, he escapes. But not from his conscience.
Thinking he sees the old guy's murdered ghost,
boyo rushes into the street. They've opened
a manhole, searching for leaking gas,
Boyo falls in; a sensational explosion,
and he quite disappears. A moral lesson.

Pity they had to use such old-fashioned music.

TELEVISING CHRISTMAS EVE

Camera One   A crowd colours the stone-grey square
                      around
                an illuminated rootless Christmas tree;
                everyone singing, as if they'd suddenly
                      found
                which hark the herald angels might set free:
                some new beginning, a clean line drawn
                beneath
                private mistakes, betrayals; what sharing a
                feast
                can briefly purify - or laying a wreath
                on a monument to the publicly deceased.

Camera Two　Curlicued high on buildings, the pink feet
　　　　　　of pigeons balance, whitening niche and
　　　　　　　　spar,
　　　　　　sheening their necks to jerk a flick-eyed view
　　　　　　over the sound of difference in the street:
　　　　　　creatures who don't know where or what
　　　　　　they are
　　　　　　peering at those below who think they do.

AT THE DENTIST

He peered inside my mouth. *Not bad for your age.*
They'll see the rest of you out. As if to gage
his prophecy, he probed their rooted core.
This one needs filling. Reached for, the chromium arm
the drill suspended from was pulled near
as, open-mouthed, I swallowed moist alarm.
I want to pick your brains now I've got you here,
Jill, my assistant's, newly hooked on reading.
Collins and Archer. What should she try next?
'Urgh ... argh ... ,' I offered. *Reading's so improving.*
Should she try Christie? Or perhaps Jean Plaidy?
'Argh ... urgh ... ,' I volunteered. *Funny or moving,*
it must be clean enough for a young lady.
The suction tube removed, the treatment ended,
'I hope,' I said, 'she enjoys what I've recommended.'

WORD OVER ALL
(An Old Reporter Files His Story On His Hundredth Burns Supper)

I: Before

Tartan tables drape the room
where artificial thistles bloom,
tapped mikes are tested - *boom, boom, boom.*
All is then ready to receive
guests who'll arrive in droves to weave
what for an evening they'll believe;
that history itself adjourns
while they, with amateurish turns,
affect the memory of Burns.

A piper's bag, alive with air,
scraiching a march leads, pair by pair,
the folk who'll people the affair;
be-kilted, buckled, tartan-sashed,
with wealth and reputation stashed
and settled self-importance fashed,
they scrape out chairs amid a hum
of chat, then settle, bum by bum,
expectantly; politely dumb
as, memory raxed across his face,
the chairman chants the Selkirk Grace,
and waitressed soup pervades the place.

II: During

Polite spoon clatters tepid plate;
the hired teen-agers congregate
to swoop, upon a given sign,
and clear the tables, pour the wine.

Outside the hall a bagpipe's groan
heralds the haggis, held up, shown
beribboned on a silver ashet.
A callow youth prepares to gash it,
but first pours out the fiery dram
that warms the piper's diaphragm;

then, waving a Balmoral dirk,
cuts up the metre of the work
you, Burns, once uttered to the haggis
whose native fare the well-filled bag is.
Done hashing your addressing verses,
skin-slashing, he, alas! disperses
more than the amber dews. A squirt
of haggis hits a neighbour's shirt.
Another, wasplike, comes to rest
upon a female's ample chest,
her pidgeoned bosom cleavage-naked.
A waitress rushes in to slake it
before it dribbles - who knows where? -
or gawpers turn around to stare.
But such mishaps are quickly finished
once the surprise first shock's diminished.

With dods of haggis, tatties, neeps,
the teetered waitresses make sweeps
down lines of tables, dropping platters
through talking shoulders; all that matters,
delivering a speedy run,
all eaten, others not begun.

Hurtled round next comes gristly beef
with Yorkshire pudding and a sheaf
of vegetables from the vice
of a deep-freezer. Now, the ice
of conversation's melted too -
I'm so-and-so. And who are you?

Next, tinned fruit-salad follows on,
then coffee and a sweet bon-bon.
The first toast raised, *God Bless the Queen*,
and distant faces, sharply seen,
grow quickly blurred behind blue smoke
that screens flushed face or dubious joke.

A song begins the entertainment;
a tenor, tight in his containment,
squeezes an empty toothpaste sound

as phrases rallentando round
familiarity, and hands
tap sympathies no Scot withstands.

An old man, bouncing self-esteem
from specs that flash a gold-rimmed gleam,
expatiates on wives and mothers
with sentiment that safely smothers
the flaring quarrels each day brings
since she and he were kings and queens,
their coupling ruling him a god
who thought he'd moved the earth's cold sod
some forty stranging years ago.
(Her blush, recalling, nods *Just so!*)
But ah! time thickens as it passes -
with shaky hand he toasts *The Lasses*.

The limping 'Star o' Rabbie Burns' -
sickly the sentiments it churns! -
precedes the settling in the seat
guest speakers, rising to their feet,
are greeted with to show respect
for such an honoured intellect.

As priests, inventing sects and churches,
shaped prejudice that still besmirches
all superstitions but their own -
belief's a fierce contentious bone! -
so the august Burns Federation,
secure in its renowned oblation
of Burns above all other scribes
(especially verse with living vibes)
prescribes the order of the praise
for use upon Burns-holy-days,
ensuring the official version
is what receives world-wide dispersion.

Their gold-chained speaker who uprises
sermons us platitudes, surmises,
his voice with worshipped fervour misted
speaks on, as if our Bard existed

without traditions gone before;
his metres, stanzas, Scottish lore
a splendid isolated peak
past, present, future needn't seek
to challenge or to emulate;
much like the ship-in-bottle state
of Scotland, sailing forth on myth
reality has no truck with.

He speaks of Burns, the common man
with sympathies that overran
the wisest, wittiest superhuman
who ever lifted leg on woman.
He speaks of Burns, the social drinker
whom whisky made a lofty thinker;
of Burns, the radical, defending
the poor whose plight seems never-ending;
of Burns the this, and Burns the that,
assuming what he would be at;
which join and who support, could he
return, a living mortgagee.
Meanwhile, the most must just be made
of honouring his sacred shade -
a kind of secular Jesus Christ
with whom Scots keep an annual tryst.

As words that roll round nothing said
bid inattention think of bed,
or holidays, or just go sifting
the loosened ends thoughts trail when drifting,
his listeners were in boredom lost
before he reached the ringing toast,
But, as exhorted, each upstanding -
save those with knees long past commanding -
half-hushed in odoured sanctity,
clinked The Immortal Memory,
sat down, all concentration sapped,
but long and loudly cheered and clapped,
with, here and there, a *hic* or *horum*
from those who'd drunk a muckle jorum.

More songs and recitations followed
with whisky-watered patience swallowed
as on and on the ritual wended
until, with *Auld Lang Syne*, it ended.

III: After

Then out the congregation edges,
already patriotic pledges
forgotten. Puzzled by direction,
some walk with airy circumspection;
some urgent for relief; some laggard;
some charged with new-found zeal; some haggard;
each to his isolation goes,
some to face icy words or snows;
others, the police's breathalizer
leaving them many months the wiser.

Mindful of editorial pleadings,
I, to report on the proceedings,
then , with a glass of smooth Bowmore
in silent reading re-explore
the poetry you only hear
when sounded on the inner ear,
and man to man (or woman) speaks
eternities beyond critiques.

Movements and causes rise and fall
while human cruelties appal.
What thing lives on? Word over all.

MR LONELYHEART

For the umpteenth rush-hour time he stalked the railway
station clock, clutching the *Telegraph*,
this 'well-preserved, successful entrepreneur,
good-looking, theatre-loving, youthful forty,
eager to share his assets with a lady
of similar interests'.

What the plain girl
saw was a worn, bespectacled, obese
bald-headed man, exuding lack of charm
and greased in sweat. Shrinking into the crowd,
the nearest trash-can gulped her *Telegraph*.

He watched the Gothic hands of the clock jerk
minute from emptied minute, till the bounds
of possibility got ticked beyond
the furthest reach of chance. Shrugging his collar,
to shield accustomed anonimity,
he shuffled back to sexual fantasy.
The next advert, who knows, might do the trick.

A CARPET

He felt the stress of parting when they came,
shirt-sleeved, broad-chested, one a little lame,
to lift the carpet, worn beyond reclaim -
nothing survives the fabric's wear and tear -

and lay a new one on the naked floor,
close-fitted, from the windows to the door,
over the chipped surround, varnished before,
stretching fresh waves of comfort down the stair.

He watched them as they prised tacks, tight with rust,
strip underfelting like a broken crust
spread with a lair of deeply trampled dust
that coughed acridity upon the air;

rip up the carpet where he once had trod
bare-footed childhood through; and, later, shod,
decided that there couldn't be a God,
since adolescence hurt and wasn't fair.

And on the underside noticed the stain
of beer he'd spilled when, hard against the grain,
he'd wrestled with first love; but all in vain;
her virgin caution making her not dare.

Much later, on the couch where he'd proposed
true happiness, four wooden feet had nosed
their weight into the pile. Newly exposed
were claw-like indentations, canvas-bare.

Reproaches, arguments and tardy praise,
both good and bad, and best-forgotten days
when baffled blind by chance's losing phase,
had fixed the carpet with his sightless stare.

He'd played across it as his children grew;
when age engulfed him, seen the threadless cue
that much uncertained what he'd thought he knew
before he came to grapple with despair.

Long after love had satisfied its bed
and tenderness lay calmly in its stead,
what poetry must say had all been said,
the deaf world turned its back and didn't care,

having its own raw problems - racked by greed
and wars, the hapless cry of human need -
to which the folk who ran it paid scant heed,
recklessly thinning off its ozone layer.

The carpet he'd thus cushioned life upon,
rolled up, high-shouldered to destruction gone,
urged that he shared the same criterion:
nothing survives the fabric's wear and tear.

DIVORCED

What was it fractured their relationship?
Her fault? A prudish holding-back in bed?
A shoulder weighted with some dressed-up chip?
Intolerance? Ignoring what he said?

Or was it his? A business that exhausted?
Or playing on the side with newer women?
Fragmenting casualness he hadn't costed?
Or not accepting life's routinely human?
A walking silence broken at the edges,
he shops for one, cracks supermarket jokes;
has access to his kids through legal pledges;
connects in passing with a *how're ya, folks;*
in washaterias gazing at his laundry,
as if its churn might rinse his lonely quandary.

ON CERTAIN ACADEMIC POETS

He criticised our inadequacies when we were young,
so we don't include him, pretend that he doesn't exist;
that'll make the bugger wish he'd never sharpened his
       tongue;
for so long as we're around he'll never be missed.

It's easy to promote ourselves and our friends
secure in the sinecure of academic niches;
we arbitrate the only true poetic ends,
exclusively approving just what each other teaches;

taking care to keep at a safe distance behind us
those who might be whetting a newer-handled knife.
Yes, of course, it's true that history may unmind us,
but meanwhile, we're the cutting edge of poetical life.

THE STROKE

Wandered within the mazed coils of his mind;
what happened only to friends felled him. A stroke.
The familiar sound of his own voice couldn't find
the way through which his usual clarity spoke.
His clouded thoughts piled up against themselves,
banking what blocked released communication,
the accustomed shapes of his consonants and vowels
trailing a groan which bore him no relation.
He heard them say: *He's lost the power of an arm,
and a side of his brain's affected.* They said: *He's not
likely to speak again. No cause for alarm.
We'll have to make the best of what he's still got.*
On the closed side of the shutter, frustrations fought;
to the other, food and embarrassed pity were brought.

OLD SIR WILLIAM

He led the pitiless fields of industry with the flash of his
name,
force-marching his abilities far beyond the common reach,
dominating sherry-tables, board-rooms, the TV game
of prophesying weekly where some unlikely probing breach
might salient recession, or strike with counter-flanking slump
and over-run the thin-held line of a too-relaxed prosperity.
He hadn't counted human figures when he came to dump
wastelands of unemployed, the campaigned casualties of
severity.
Far from the distant-sounding fronts, the forces he
commanded,
the cheque-book lunches, applauded speechy dinners, he lies
spoon-fed
on minced-up munchings, the ruthless bric-a-brac of his
dignity stranded
limply upon the rubber-sheeted stench of a wet bed,
matted with words, the worry-beads of forgotten half-
conversions.
Old age, the sprucing nurse observed, *is no respecter of persons.*

OLD FOLKS' HOME

An old man stumbled along the institutional
corridor, one end of a piece of string
tied to his finger. With his other hand
he kept pressing the free end against the wall.
Whatever are you doing?, the nursing sister
rounded the corner with. *Trying to connect*,
the old man answered, pressing the string harder.
Relaxing him with an indulgent smile,
the sister said: *Come on now, Mr Foster;*
some of the old connections no longer work.

SEPARATES

Separates, she said, *are what I'll buy.*
I remember wondering, fifty years ago,
what such a name for clothes might signify
when life's a ceaseless struggle to bestow

the idea of the unity of things
where no such unity exists. The flow
of flotsammed time, whatever else it brings,
allows no shapes of permanence to grow;

nor echoes from what's gone an Age of Gold
that somehow rubbed the spread of living's stains
clean from the fabric; nor maps space to hold
a vanished Eden, freed from loss and gain.

There's not an idling bird on singing tree
knows where it came from, nor why it should be
the bearer of its borrowed melody
that flaunts a reassuring filigree

of happiness. We thrill to music heard
between the moveless silence through which slide
our brief affections, touching or absurd,
to hold awhile together, then divide.

Warm lovers, threshed in fleshing, realise
combined release. Their moistures make them cry
rapture. But when apart their bodies prise,
they hear the sightless sound go rushing by;

the river that is not, and never was,
through country filled with distance that dissolves
in mists of nothingness, effect from cause,
all history's bravura of resolves.

Why should a placard in a fashioned sale
awaken thoughts that reach past human tears,
when, waiting, I could sink a glass of ale
and banter reassurance with my peers?

She pushed back through the crowd. *Got what you sought?*
I asked her empty hands. *No. They're sold out.*

WHIPPET FOR HIGH TEA

Heh Jimmy, listen. Here's a bluidy guid yin.
Some fucker's left a copy o *The Times*
on the table. It sez that in America, a union
of fuckan lesbians, gays an coloured people -
cunts, thae jurnalists, as if we wisnae aa coloured -
huv got together wi academicks tae pruve that
whit's written in the papers ivry day
is jist as guid as whit fuckan Wullie Shakespeare
fucked us up wi at school. Jeez, fuckan marvelluz,
en't it, Jimmy? 'Deconstructionists,'
they caa themsels. Appreciatiun at last,
eh Jimmy? 'Deconstructionists'. Whit the fuck . . .

Heh lassie, giez a pint. Pit it oan the slate.
It cannae be closin time! It's no that late?

UNFORMALISTIC SONNET

to escape the crime of
            poets like
    fourteen fractured lines
don't rhyme

                        scan
            winning freedom from
                    outmoded trad
    claim
            widens the scope of
but looks as if   parasite
    gnawing the edges
        modernistic teeth
                    leave suspicion-marks
            can't self-discipline to

GENERATION GAP

We are all born to alienation
                        R. D. Laing

Watching the players shift from human concern
to sentimental violence - 'Yarra wanny
uz; yir wanny them' - and beginning to learn
how Glasgow drunkenness makes a tough wee manny
the image we present of our Scottish kind,
soap opera, tribal football, panel games
cornered by television, light of the mind
whose silence-filling mirrors aimless aims.
Believing myself a poet who once spoke
for a country bent on healing the scars of class,
I find myself a dozer who suddenly woke
in a theatre the audience left *en masse*;
alone with the dropped curtain, the empty pit;
left-over prop from a scene that doesn't fit.

ON BEING LEFT OUT OF A SUPPOSEDLY
DEFINITIVE ANTHOLOGY

> . . . give up verse, my boy,
> There's nothing in it.
>
> Ezra Pound

Another casual snub, a wounding slight
that seems to threaten fragile poethood;
depression falls from some anonymous height.
Give the thing up: you can't be any good.
Cloudings of doubt despair, too thick to last;
play parlour games; collect for charity;
or turn yourself a bluff enthusiast
for television's forced hilarity.
I read again the best of what I've written;
the heart, I tell myself, *knows what it knows.*
However sorely petty vanity's bitten,
however wounding meaningless counterblows,
another image stirs, the game's afoot,
and poetry sets off in hot pursuit.

BOOKENDS

You don't think much about your possible ending
unless a friend, retreated out of reach,
reminds you by his exit that mind-bending
horror's forever widening its breach.
The left-hand bracket bookends up the year
that brought your birth. The right one doesn't show
room for what lies between; the hope and fear
you bind into experience as you go.
A doctor, fingering my ganglioned wrist
looked serious, sounded me, then suddenly said:
Your heart-beat is irregular: a twist
that for a moment spun me, half-afraid
the right-hand bracket seeming to equate
bookending space to prop my second date.

7.11 THE BROOMILAW: RMS *COLUMBA*

I

Hoarsely the steamer hoots; the gangway clatters;
stern-held, her bow right-angles from the quay;
bells clang; rope-lifted water drips in tatters,
as threshing paddles churn to pull her free.

Buildings get smalled to insignificance
behind her swallow-trail of sizzled lace;
the keen prow furrows into blue-hilled distance
as *Full Ahead* her thumping paddles race.

My senses, newly summered in their priding
and flowered with the privilege of my class,
(which, half-ashamed of me, won't stay in hiding)
reach out to mingle with the pluralled mass,

shaped to monotony by clock-bound toiling
at benches or machines; who, for a week,
(taut springs let loose in all-too-brief recoiling)
pursue whatever pleasure's nearest; seek

the drift and cameraderie of drinking,
or reddening skins upon a sunstrip beach,
untroubled by the burden brought by thinking
of what's concealed from common-sense's reach -

music that trembles over troubled edges;
the vasty deeps of an infinity
of feelings poetry maps words for (pledges
that apprehend their bounds, but yet run free);

philosophy, behind its clouds of reason
refuting and refining all intent;
half-shades of truth that lead the mind to seize on
some ultimate of meaning still unmeant.

But these are artificial things I'm bred to,
and don't concern the most of those we meet,
the plod of their imaginations dead to
what lies beyond the surface world, complete

in what it offers all who, in their stations,
do what they can, expecting little change
from inequalities that try their patience,
and politicians strive to re-arrange.

II

Fuming the fret of troubled adolescence,
I swore that I would tilt such wrongs to right;
teach history the logic of its lessons
and for our common human values fight.

But words like *common* baffle close defining,
and who's to set the wavered balance clear?
I spoke at bleary meetings, undermining
the very values that I held most dear;

yet found my rawhide sympathies rejected,
the cast of politic thoughts that I expressed
a coin the face of which was not acepted,
the words, the accent and the way I dressed

the suit of confidence as worn by bosses -
I was a spy, a traitor to my kind.
Not every loser knows his weight of losses
nor where they were, nor what's not there to find.

So I resolved to be a private person,
abjuring gestures palpably absurd,
free of the wind that rhetoric must rehearse on,
a poet's, not a politician's word

the sharper truth; a honing edge much keener
than promises ballooned to colour votes,
the logic of unpopular demeanour
punctured by what an opposition floats.

All that was long ago. Now, chance so ranges
its wreak of havoc, it has paid amends
to those a generation gap estranges
from us who tried and failure reprehends.

Then, as the steamer surged us towards fresh pleasures,
they to their pubs and fish-and-chips high teas:
(for satisfaction's served in different measures),
I, to my sensual thoughts where, lolled at ease,

I dreamt of girls I'd bet a winning card on
by shores that breezed a gently warming sun;
by flowers that softly waved profusive pardon
for sins I'd thought of, but had not yet done.

Empty the seas now, and the lazing garden's
part of a car-park linking two hotels,
while age's creeping spread of concrete hardens,
laying the ghosts that memory compels.

CHOOSING

(After the Archdeacon of York Minster's suggestion, broadcast in BBC Radio 4's Thought for the Day *on 15 December 1992, that Mary could have said 'No', and might not even have been the first choice.)*

First, the Archangel Gabriel hovered over Lili,
a barmaid, who shrilled his invisible voice a harsh reception:
I've never yet heard anything quite so impossibly silly!
I'm a good girl. You can keep your immaculate conception.

Next, the Archangel fluttered above a Scot, Louise:
Ah'm engaged tae a fella wha disnae like fuss ur boather
Gien a wumman a faitherless wean? Whit a kinky wheeze!
Dinna ye carrie yur hocus-pocus ony further.

So Gabriel lighted on Mary, an aged carpenter's bride
she'd marry out of pity; a kindly man who bumbled.
Wanting a child, she agreed, if Gabriel promised to hide
her in legendary myth, that Joseph wouldn't be humbled . . .

The Archangel duly reported: *Done, of her own free will;*
leaving mankind free to choose to make wars and kill.

LULLABY FOR AN AMERICAN GRANDSON
(for Conner Maurice Gavin Bell)

Go to sleep, my baby, close your pretty eyes,
though no roving angels lace protective skies,
innocently praising God with emptied songs.
Now the world you're born to rings with ancient wrongs,
half-forgotten hatreds, festering tribal scars;
profiteering weapons itching mindless wars;
dizzied hordes of frenzies, disrespecting laws,
bent on killing others for some factless cause;
promises for breaking, pacts not meant for keeps;
drought, starvation quicken; exiled pity weeps.

Go to sleep, my baby, close your beaming eyes;
one day when you waken you will realise
pomped religions quarrel over man-made creeds,
powerless to succour bleeding human needs.
If, as Tolstoy uttered, life is meaningless
since no supernatural force can hear or bless,
we must make a meaning as we go along,
reasoning for rightness, weak against the strong;
we must make our meaning, shape an attitude
that resists all dogma, as a thinker should.

Go to sleep, my baby, may those eager eyes
penetrate deceptions, politicians' lies;
may the faults of others trapped within the mire
of their own frustration, not make tolerance tire.
Disappointments shadow self-esteem with pain;

from despair's engulfing struggle free again.
Moons are not for crying; what you can't achieve,
green no wastes of envy, nor let longing grieve.
Worlds are not for saving, do what best you can;
human flesh breeds troubles time itself can't span.

Go to sleep, my baby, close your dreaming eyes.
One day, baffled *wherefores* and bewildered *whys*
will reveal some answers, true a little while.
May they bring you judgement, wit, a kindly style;
power brokered justly, not on others' fears,
leadershipping courage not misled by cheers.
Cradling love enfolds you; may it grow your own,
sharing with another strength not yours alone.
May acceptance season all the senses bring,
gratitude and wonder gracing everything.

A CHRISTMAS TREE

Three children cluster around the Christmas tree, a
    confection
newly assembled, pleased with their branched collection
        of reindeer, santas, baubles and fairy lights,
anticipation eagering its reflection.

How about making a christmas wish? I idly suggest,
thinking that brightly each of them might request
        some lusted-after toy, or a gadget for pleasure.
Anxieties, not desires, were what they expressed.

The youngest said: *What's the point of hosted angelic peace*
when everywhere furtive men make war, release
        death on innocent children much like us?
Why doesn't God stop bombing, have killing cease?

The second angrily blurted: *Protection for the whale*
and all other creatures whose line could easily fail
        if their habitat is polluted, or they get hunted,
defenceless flesh and bone broken up for sale.

Puzzled, the third protested: *Why isn't the ozone layer*
respected by every nation; allowed repair
        the damage ignorant selfishness has inflicted?
Tarnishing earth for us children isn't fair.

Whatever could I wish when finally my turn came?
My qualifying excuses sounded lame
        to them. *You started it,* they accused, *you must say!*
I mumbled. Was my generation wholly to blame

for the shameful uncauses that lead to a waste of innocence
    spilt,
yet which politicians had seen as windmills to tilt
        at safely; an easy brush with disposable words?
Surely they were the ones who must wear the guilt? . . .

The likes of me couldn't know the half-truths that
    pragmatize choice
when jobs and profits threaten the equipoise
        of nature, balancing probabilities? . . .
Only children speak with a shadowless voice.

MAKING WARS

I

Man, said Goethe, needs to believe in something
outside himself. The catalogue is endless,
fashioned for true believers; foolproof, bendless
against the breath of argument if you sing
total conviction, swallowing faith in doses
so that it saturates and saps the senses,
dulling the cutting-edge of reason; fences
exclusiveness, a pasture of tame supposes.
It may be a god with a big or little 'g',
or a cause unfurling hatred like a flag;
dogma that makes mere human pity sag
helpless before such mindless certainty.
You pay your prejudice and fake your choice,
tuning the silence to your fancied voice.

II

Boys, scarecely off their footballs, prowl the streets
brandishing weapons like the nursery toys
they cut their teeth on playing soldier-men;
sallies to fire at movement, then retreats
behind the stubs of ruins, with the noise
of shells crumping on shoppers, killing - ten? -
the number doesn't matter. Pity blunts
itself upon such massed brutality
that murders reason and the ghosts of shame.
Turned schizophrenic, human nature hunts
the mirror-image of its sanity,
the deaths of others to these boys, a game,
ejaculating guns on mindless air,
ripping the lining stitched against despair.

III

Where do they come from, all these bombs and guns,
burgeoning camouflage like buds in Spring?
Who trains the men to sally armoured runs
through decent, ordered foreign streets and bring
death and destuction, like some bibled plague,
blinding small babies, blasting children's legs
to salvage ancient hatreds, blurred and vague,
while helpless pity weeps and hunger begs?
Robe-shadowed whispers, side-mouthed dividends
with patriotic profits - jobs for the boys -
and civilising governments whose ends
purvey defence. If that, perchance, destroys,
then clearly, blame must lie with those who buy it,
and not the men of honour who supply it.

IV

Cleansed from their ethnic villages by gains
the enemy shelled and looted, left the clothes
disaster shivers in, they drift to plains
of hopelessness across our armchairs. Those
with charity for conscience see the stains
of tears and reach for cheque-books, but oppose
absorbing vagrant misery. *No,* explains
the politician. *People can't be transposed.*
Better leave them where they are and send
them medicine, food and blankets. They'll return
one day to where they came from; try to mend
the broken fences. Nailing his concern
against the stable doors of TV screens,
viewers half-nod. Of course they know what he means.

WHY

You say the attack was mindless? Not quite so.
Think of the pressures building up inside
the brain of a fellow made by nature slow,
inadequacies lacking a lie to hide
in, backward at learning, with no *à propos*
to relate to; one who'll never feel the pride
of a job well done, the force of work his foe,
fending him off across its bleak divide.
He sees around rich 'haves' with their purpose shot
and more than a share of the goodies he, too, desires;
exiled to deprivation, a hopeless 'have not'
in god-abandoned wasteland. Frustration fires
the explosive charge - what can't be won might be taken.
No wonder respectable heads get gravely shaken.

A ROUGH DAY

It blew up somewhere behind the weather-man's
computerised cloud-patches, gliding slowly
across the television screen, shafted
by thickened arrows. Suddenly, we're its reach.

Invisible stabbings whistle past my face,
collaring head-down up the glen, my rufflered
dogs snuffling the ghosts of life from sodden
leaf-mould layers; what's left of trampled summer.

Then, the trinkling burn was crystal chatter,
unrippling clearness, draping its allegory
of stillness over the ledge above the pool.
Now, dissolving shifts of snow drop distance

sheer on the gully, levering peated soil
powdery loose; clutching at broken limbs
of branches, boating the skeletal veins of bracken;
a gulp, try as it will, that wouldn't swallow.

Trees splinter the creak of their years and fall
like fronds, like friends ... *Thank goodness,* I tell myself,
angled to earth, *I'm not of this hurry;*
merely the testing-ground for to-morrow's quarry.